DARK STONES I CARRIED

WILLIS McCREE

Copyright ©2020 Willis McCree

All rights reserved.

ISBN: 978-1-7342049-2-6
Library of Congress Control Number: 2020901897

All rights reserved. No part of this book may be reproduced, stored in a retrieval system, or transmitted in any form or by any means without prior written permission from the author, except for the use of brief quotations in a book review.

Edited by Jonathan Clark
Cover design by Judith S. Design & Creativity
www.judithsdesign.com
Published by Glass Spider Publishing
www.glassspiderpublishing.com

J-W-J

Secrets kept in the dark control us; in the light they have no power. I set mine free and in so doing, myself.

ACKNOWLEDGMENTS

Gratitude to Tim Grethers, LCSW who saved my life and helped me find my true self.

Thanks to Jonathan Clark for his keen eye and sense of balance that has helped give this work its true voice.

Love to John Fromer who keeps pushing me to bring forth words, and to Jacob Gallegos who keeps teaching me to let go.

TABLE OF CONTENTS

INTRODUCTION:
YESTERDAY WAS A SAD DAY 11

SECTION I: YESTERDAY
THE SCAR 15
PENMANSHIP 17
THE SIDE OF THE ROAD 19
DRIP DROP 21
CHRISTIAN CHARM CAMP 22
THE ATTIC BOARDS 24
TOBACCO AND SEWAGE 26
MONEY FOR ROSES 27
TO THE DOGS 29
SILENCE 31
MY FATHER'S EYES 34
COMES THE STORM 36
A HOUSE ILLUMINATED 38

SECTION II: ME OR THE MASK I WEAR?
NO ANSWER 43
THE PARALLEL UNIVERSE OF CARY GRANT 44
SLAPPED AWAY 46
DEMONS 48
BLACKNESS 49
IN MY GARAGE 51

THE WRONG DEATH	53

SECTION III: ALL THE WRONG PLACES

SAND BAR	57
SHATTERED BONES	59
FATIGUES	60
CURTAINS	62
SHEETS	64
MIRAGE	65
PASTELS	66
SEEKING PROOF	67
IT RINGS	69

SECTION IV: BACKSTAGE

THE LOFT	73
IF THE MORNING COULD CHANGE	75
I TRIED TO TELL YOU	77
THE YEAR OF REPENTANCE	79

EPILOGUE: TO THE LIGHT

TOMORROW IS HERE	83

INTRODUCTION

YESTERDAY

"Do you have patience to wait till your mud
settles and the water is clear?"
(Lao Tzu)

YESTERDAY WAS A SAD DAY

Dark clouds pulled over my eyes
like the sheets of my unmade bed,
keeping out the light,
the people, pain.

Sick. Days without
an appetite, food.
My days, nights spent with
vodka thickening my brain.

A month since I buried my mother—
Muddy knees, hands on the steel-blue dome,
loss—another loss added
onto heaps I already carry.

Dirty feet, crawled in the backyard.
The shotgun on the floor
a dead dog, hangover.
The bang cleaves the skull.

Laying curled on the couch—
In my womb of darkness,
a stillborn fetus.

SECTION I

RAGES AND RABID DOGS

"You can be full of kindness and love, but you
cannot sleep next to a mad dog."
(Ashin Wirathu)

THE SCAR

His grandfather was an IRA explosives
expert. His father, a coal miner. He caught
snakes for the university, worked the mines.

Lost his mother early. Stole food to survive
the depression. Hated
Dagos—I was 23
before I knew what that was.

Dropped women like
flies. Grey, green eyes—
pierced their hearts.
Took them into a sea of sex,
drowned them and let their
spent bodies wash up on his shore.

Bib overalls, work shoes, and a railroad cap,
that's all he wore—my father.
Gaped open, showing his slender
sides shining like a bronze sea.

Dirty hands from work, and a tormented
mind. A combination that made him irresistible
to me—to others. Crashed

his car into the neighbor's wife's,
wearing those overalls.
She was wearing
less. We had to move,
get a new car.

Mother cried a lot
and drank a lot
in those days.

His anger, directed, released —
I hear the snap of
his belt, feel
the sting of
a scar.

PENMANSHIP

A poet trapped
inside a farm boy—
Too pretty for overalls, but
forced to wear them anyway.

Forced to do
so many things,
accept so many things.
Never accepting myself,
never quite normal.

Assignment, write a poem.
New at this school—No one
knew the secrets of home
or how I wrote.

A poem about Paul Bunyan.
Words slanting left like
windblown sassafras trees
by the barn.

The teacher didn't approve of left handers.
Evidence held high,
shamed me. Was I
the only one?

One hand forced to sleep, the other
to write flowing curves
and letters slanting to the right.
My brain confused. I was confused.

The note from the teacher
brought the belt, slashing
cutting to the left like
the slant of my l's.
Blood in his eyes, on the floor.

THE SIDE OF THE ROAD

They found me on the road side,
these passersby.
A bloody mess
curled inside itself.

Blackened eyes, split lips,
blood and snot dripping from my nose.
The truck I drove still running,
parked on the graveled shoulder.

Door still open,
engine still grinding
where I jumped out
as my mother's head was smashed

through the side window
of the car in front of me.
My father's hand
pushed her through it.

His fists pounded her face
until I pulled her away.
Then I
took her place.

He foamed at the mouth
like the rabid dog
I shot the week before,
standing on the front porch.

All this because she got drunk
at Edith's Tupperware party.
Country hens who couldn't handle
a beautiful, blonde drunk.

DRIP DROP

Pellets of rain spray leaves,
bullet sounds plinking in my ears
like it did the first time I was forced
by the boy
from the dairy farm down the road.

If the rain goes silent, I will cut.
Cut where no one can see
drip drop splashes of red,

Not rain,

covering up screams
of a terrified boy
who cannot stop
the flow.

If I cut, I won't feel the other pain.

I won't bleed there.

I won't call his name, beg him to stop.

I won't like it after all.

I will pray the rain keeps
drip dropping.

CHRISTIAN CHARM CAMP

Church, scriptures, and the Good Lord will help you.
"Won't they, son?" the reverend asked.
"Yes sir, reverend," my reply.
Mother silent as the bible commands,
looked up toward heaven.
Father smiled, signed waivers, wrote a check.

Sent to Summer Youth Conference—
or Christian Charm Camp (CCC) as I would later name it.
Designed to help troubled youth,
conversion experiences for the
unclean—
abominations according to Leviticus.

At camp, other boys who
practiced evil—
Relegated to bible study, prayer, group activities
to help us
turn to righteous living.

A prank with my toothpaste.
Curse words on the counselor's door
where I stood—

Naïve, honest, not the culprit.
My nickname, Country.

Naivete is a strong intoxicant.
People so easily fall.
Wasn't it what Cary Grant used
to get the girl, to have people love him?
A perfect mask to wear.

I used it to charm the pants off the counselor.
CCC the first step,
left camp silent about the counselor
and
a little less Country.

THE ATTIC BOARDS

On two wide boards
in an attic summer heat so hot
mice abandoned it.
In winter, icicles formed on the rafters.

My angry father jailed me there
due to some childhood mishap—
One of his Masonic mementoes
or some rule broken.

He spit foam, yelled obscenities,
hit me, his belt
whipping, scarring.

When bleeding began, he
stopped—
Red rivulets, reminders
of his anger.

Later, taking the blade
from his Gillette razor.
Tiny cuts.
My skin separates and bleeds.

I'd leave blood on the blade,
return it for him to use,
hoping he'd be calm.
He wasn't.

I put on my mask
in that attic—became someone else.
Pain and shame couldn't take me.

It gave me power—
Drive—courage: to leave the hills,
have an early marriage, move
away.

Lost to a life being someone else,
someone trying to control
addiction and all within it.
The work of a home and family.
No life for me. Tried
to make an impossible life possible

become someone who would do
anything to please, get love,
keep peace, not search for
blades or bake in an attic,
just act the way others wanted.

TOBACCO AND SEWAGE

Day was hot, sticky like
tobacco leaves. I moved through
the patch
removing sucker growth
so the leaves grew bigger. A chore

my brother and I had
before Daddy got home.
I'd done my half, my brother hadn't.
I went back to the house, laid out
in the backyard.

Naked, free and calm.
He arrived

grabbed me, whipped me with a limb,
slashed my naked body. Threw me
into the path of the septic—
flies and waste.

I crawled out.
He pushed me back to the yard. The light
gone out of the sky.

"Only a lazy piece of shit
lays around in the sun."

MONEY FOR ROSES

He slapped me black and blue
the morning I asked for money
to buy flowers
for the girl from school.

She was in the hospital,
and I was sweet on her.
Masonic ring cut my eye.
Bit my tongue.

After his fists hit my stomach,
pee ran down my leg
into my shoe—
Later, blood.

I stole roses
from a neighbor's yard,
wrapped them,
took them to the hospital.

She said thanks.
She wasn't sweet on me.
I wanted her, someone, a man
to love me.

A dog at the foot of my father's bed,
waiting for master's love.
A hurt, loyal brute of a boy
who never asked for money again.

TO THE DOGS

We stood together, brother-sister pillars on a porch
in graying twilight
and watched stars pop out like pimples on our young faces.

Bright stars shining over us, our parents
lost in another world of addiction and violence,
leaving us alone, afraid, abandoned.

Your hunger gnawed your stomach
even after I shot the rabid dog
that chased you, as if
you were a brittle bone he wanted to chew.

His skull blown away, exposing jaw bones.
A limp, bloodied carcass
in the grass, staring at us
with no face.

Inside, I fried chicken, boiled potatoes,
and tried to make milk gravy
from greasy drippings left in the skillet.

No milk, all the cows were dry—waiting to drop calves.
Our mother's milk gone too, like her—
dried up and withered away.
I blended water, flour, grease, chicken bits.

The more I stirred, the thicker it got,
until I could stir no more.
It was not gravy.

Like dogs we ate chicken and potatoes
in dark silence and wondered
if we would see tomorrow burn down on us.

Outside, the dog choked on the skillet muck.
We opened the faucet
shoved the garden hose down her throat.

She ran away,
tail between her legs. We laughed, then cried
and went back into the dark house.

SILENCE

In the silence of the house,
no creaking, no wind, no sleep,
hoping she'd come home,
but
no car drove up.
Milking the cows in the quiet dark next morning.
"Sook, sook, sook cows," they'd already lined up
waiting
to have their swollen udders drained.

My hands chapped and aching, I
get my little sister off to school.
Tell everyone
"I took too long to milk.
Don't talk about this,"
something she'd remember later.

A hitchhike into town
to find our mother —
drunk,
needing to go somewhere,
be with someone. Later,
when I drank, I needed those things too.

Twenty-six miles in a stranger's car.
Silent.
Her car was parked at the bar on the State Line Road
the "Dixie something or other"
with its rebel flag over the door.

Its roofline
lit
by yellow bulbs dimmed, stained
by fly shit, splashed dirt from the last rain storm.
The green Gran Torino waiting,
silent like me.
Panties
wrinkled on its floor with MacDonald's wrappers.

Inside the bar, she sits
with a good ole' boy, bottles of Bud,
shots of whiskey
her eyes shiny polished blue stones.
She stands
and comes with me. He tells her to go.
Her purse empty but for the silence—silent like me,
like her.

She's buckled in, panties underfoot
stained, wet
testament of her pride, hurt,
whatever
traded for drinks to laugh, cry,
hide her pain.
A little boy driving
homeward. A silent heap beside him.

I clean up last night's mess
and the mess I
helped into the house.
Both knowing
there is no need to talk—
Our silence
says it
all.

MY FATHER'S EYES

Sometimes when I look in the mirror
I see my father's eyes —
the blue green like ocean water,
froths, foams,
washes over me like sea rocks and sand.

I don't like seeing him there
within me —
pain of the past
sitting on the bathroom counter
next to the razor.

My broken nose looks
to the left in dark,
silent reflection.
For days I avoid the mirror, shaving.

Inherited good looks
show.
I want no part of them.
I tear at my face,

try to rip it off, turn away.
Sometimes in the mirror
I see my father's eyes,

take out the razor blade,
make red lines flow
up,
down my arms.
Blood—
quiets my father's eyes.

COMES THE STORM

A storm brews.
I hear it on the wind,
running down the ridge,
sweeping across fescue laden fields—
verdant patches sliced
by a rocky, gravel road.

Thunderheads of dust rise,
snaking through corn fields.
Rust colored clay everywhere
as a car races toward me
frozen
in the cab of the flat-bed truck

parked in the driveway.
Milk cans tethered. Bales
of hay loaded like
toppled tombstones.

The cows bellow—beg
to be fed and milked.
The car stops. A man
deposits my mother in the driveway,
drives away.

I step out, pick up
this fragile bird, put
her skeletal 90 pounds in the truck,
make my own rusty thunderheads.

Get her to the barn
before my father gets home
to avoid the thunder he brings.

There's time to sober up
puddled in the dark corner of the stanchion.
The cows ignore her—

A HOUSE ILLUMINATED

We lived in a house illuminated by
anger, aggression and alcohol.
Daddy, Mother, Sister, Brother
held constantly in its light.

Day, night, anytime—
we never knew when
the lights would go out or
the house turn cold.

Rugs full of dust and dammits too,
never cleaned or straightened,
just lying there,
unable to move.

Like me—unable to get away,
trodden on and shaken, never good enough
or strong enough
or lovely enough.

Good for one thing—
to be underfoot,
to be looked down upon
or ignored.

We lived in a house heated by
abuse, arguments and addiction—
warmed by explosions
of violence.

Windows covered with blinds.
In the winter, sheets of plastic
to keep out the cold, others.

A picture-perfect family
beaten to comply, please
and be silent.

SECTION II

ME OR THE MASK I WEAR?

"We are all wandering the earth, alone, longing
to be longed for."
(William C. Hannan)

NO ANSWER

You didn't kiss me
last you held my hand
say you love me,
no matter the type of man.
Be proud,
happy to call me son.

My tears—
torrents, fury,
seeking why you
let me take the fall.
Pretending I deserved the hurt,
the pain yours.

No kiss as you lay dying,
forehead scarred from
the wreck long ago.
Coffin closed.
Straightened your starched blue dress.

Stop the screams
abandon them
like you
abandoned me.

THE PARALLEL UNIVERSE OF CARY GRANT

When I walk backwards—
mirrored halls of time
see how I was.

Stand, stare, brightened mirrors
rooms filled with cosmetics, flowers
paparazzi just outside, eager
to see, photograph.

On set, my mask
protects me, as it did
at camp, the attic, in bed.

Let's me be in Palm Springs,
poolside with Randolph Scott,
at home among the Joshua Trees.

I continue on stage—
away from who I am,
where I am parallel.

Emerge, Cary Grant:
suave, debonair, handsome, revered.
A space traveler,
lost outside a galaxy called Hollywood.
Glitter, glamour, sweat and tears.

Everyone wears an actor's mask
to cover up the truth.

SLAPPED AWAY

Streaks of ink, morning sky,
across my mind
thoughts of you leaving.
On the porch,
where I was all night.
Had to hurt myself.
You drove away, abandoned.

They lingered, voices saying
I cannot know love.
Love the idea of love, fall quickly
into that cozy bed.

Slammed against a concrete wall.
Not good enough.
Cripples, strays, damaged
flock to my door.

Mend them, give them love,
watch them move away.
Say I won't beg,
But
then I do.

One kind word,
affirmation, compliment,
or hell, just sex.
Want me, use me,
it's all good.

Bad love is better
than no love.
Always
I bend my rules,
give love to
have it slapped away.

DEMONS

Hear the demons
outside my window,
salivating, waiting to
tear my flesh, spit it on the ground.

Demons from the past.
My father left them for me.
Chains, whips beat my naked flesh.
Failures around my neck—
throw me in a lake to drown.

Standing in the bathroom,
a familiar drip drop,
being forced.
Leaky faucet I couldn't fix.
Mirrored reflections—gray, green eyes.
Can't do anything right. "Be normal,"
my father said.

Demons whisper in my ears: things
I should have been, a father,
husband,
Christian,
more.

BLACKNESS

Saw her yesterday,
a dark demon,
black marauder.
Drove by a wreck.

Little children, a mom.
Closed my eyes,
saw us all in the carnage,
but she was there, waved.

As easy as the wind blows
a silken tent,
she slid into the seat beside me,
went home with me,

followed inside,
reminded me of glass slivers
picked from my scalp—
drunken mother driving.

We survived, but
down the hallway
I hear her say
"pain is good,"

as she writes a note,
a death sentence
already pronounced. Me,
the only one who
doesn't know.

IN MY GARAGE

Searched for dents on the car.
Blood, scrapes, stones,
a death, a crash—
I wouldn't know.

I remember unkind words,
yellow road reflectors,
darkness.
Found the street, gate, garage.

At dinner, drinks,
a request.
Lost a friendship for saying no.
Fear now of the police
knocking on the door—

another life ruined.
Weeks drag by,
no indications of an accident.

Still arrested by fear,
I could be waiting arraignment,
vehicular manslaughter or worse.
Aching head, hangover,

Broken heart, loss.
Said they were monogamous but
asked me to join.

Lies, made cheap.
Trust broken apart,
let them hurt me,
hurt myself.

THE WRONG DEATH

Timing and execution crucial.
All the ones left behind
could never know the laid-out plan
to end my life, leave my wife.

Had gone too far to go back.
Fallen in love.
Church and family would never know.
Shame drove me down that road

to the edge of destruction.
12-hour shifts, long days at school,
told everyone how tired I was.
When I drove in front of the semi,
I'd have fallen asleep.

Babies with their father gone,
a widow, all would mourn
but be spared truth:
gay, no longer worthy.

Hit loose gravel,
spun as the semi hit,
tore the bumper.
I was down the road before
it stopped.

Hid my truck till morning.
Drove to school.
Called in the hit and run.
The wife never knew.

Called the shrink,
removed my mask, showed
him the real me.
Attempted suicide, failed.

Instead, I killed the marriage.

SECTION III

ALL THE WRONG PLACES

"An obstacle is often a stepping stone."
(William Prescott)

SAND BAR

Ran aground this morning—
slow and easy morning.
Still like silvery, silent water.
From nowhere, the sandbar,
as I turned,
rammed head on,
stopped.

Asked for jazzy, easy
going music matching
the slow flow
I seemed to be.
Instead, 2 hours of TV vampire violence.

Made your breakfast.
You,
lost in fangs,
blood, raw sex.

I downed vodka shots
to keep from screaming.
Lack of respect,
total immersion
away from me.
More shots,

a sandbar.
I sat alone in the same room.
I'd wait for higher tide,
the television to stop,
hangover to begin,
pain.

SHATTERED BONES

My feet alone.
Imprints of yours in
emerald grass.
Gone, yours are gone.
Don't dare look up.
Afraid I'll see the
empty yard around me.

Holding a bag of lies, broken promises.
Wishes, river rocks.
Tell me the leash is too short.
Won't admit your lies,
wouldn't change,
give up the past
to a life of love, goodness.

Hadn't seen
how ridiculous I was.
You took, scattered my broken bones,
left me on the back lawn.
Picnic, uneaten.
Wine, undrunk. Sandwiches
spoiling in summer sun.

FATIGUES

My sister cries, stands at the door.
A U.S. Army van
running, waiting.
Left to fend alone now,

four days after graduation.
Destination: Fort Leonard Wood, Missouri.
Only left Kentucky twice.
Once to Missouri,
National FFA Convention—Kansas City.
My first taste of real love,
the boy from Louisiana
let me borrow his shorts, swam at the Y.
The second—Texas, an armadillo who died.

Standing in line,
boxer shorts, other men
getting shots, haircuts,
fatigues.
Lines of fatigues,
sweat,
the smell of men.

Seventeen, shivering, afraid
of what lies within

and what lies beyond
the next dark open door.
My life changed
from the hills
where mother lives, where life was.
It gives me hope.
Broken as the
drill sergeant yells,
"Fall in line."

In line,
push the shoulder of the next man.
Why does he have to move away?
Stay,
stay close,
don't leave like my father, the others.
Seventeen, shivering, afraid,
knowing I need to be among fatigues
and
the smell of men.

CURTAINS

Day draws the curtains.
In the lonely apartment
waiting,
having wine, too much.

Contractor arrives, estimates,
has wine, buries his face
against me. I
rise to fill his needs,

draw the curtains.
Pray you don't come home early,
see them drawn,
smell the scent of sex.

I inhale,
primal sound, lust,
one brief moment:
sunlight, fireworks flood in.

The world bright,
curtain opened,
alive again.

Wish it were you
who buries his face,
surrenders beneath me.
Those curtains you have drawn.

You come home. Curtains open.
We sit, silent, stare—
you toward the TV,
me toward another goodbye.

SHEETS

The sun rises, drips like
hot butter.
I feel it, my eyes
covered in a worn out used-tire bed.

Stained, shredded sheets.
Pillows long since
reduced, desiccated granules.
Rose cane buried in your thigh.
Bandaged you, comatose.
Didn't even know
you fell into the rosebush.
Drugs and alcohol.

Bled everywhere,
barely missing femoral artery.
Need to cut my flesh.
More spots, blood on the sheets.

I lay here,
slice, ponder.
Roar of abandonment—
a rose cane in my hand.

MIRAGE

Fell yesterday
on my way to tell you a
devastating, hollow truth.
The boy from the restaurant.

Fell at your feet,
my arms around your legs,
drank, sweet scent.

My eyes closed. Your tattoo,
ink carved, rounded mounds,
downy hair.
Realized, it was his tattoo.

Tears on your toes.
Pain, shame
you have not known,
cannot be told.
Your passion dried,
cancer
pushed it into the past.

PASTELS

I sit draped in the silky crepe
of a lavender morning.
A Von Furstenberg background,
leaves, twigs, sky.

Smokey haze from the valley,
pink, gray, invisible,
thin, wispy, stone cold
winter morning.

Months since your death—
overdose, cocaine, and rum.
The dog cremated too.
Joined you in the cemetery.
Visited yesterday,
cold, icy footsteps in snow.

Dripping icicles
shrinking from the roof,
dying a slow, warm death.
How I envy them. My death
will be violent, quick,
no witness, life's liquid
dripping onto the ground.
Laid a rose cane on the stone.

SEEKING PROOF

Woke early with the thought.
It glowed, a light I hadn't turned on.
The day grew, dawned in my mind.
I knew I'd do it. Arguments
I had with myself
gnawed at me, a bone for a starving dog.
A thousand reasons not to go.
I had to know: alcohol, drugs
gone, used with someone else.

Prepared for what I'd find,
confront you, accuse you,
make you ashamed. I was shamed.

Had to prove I was right.
You, red sunken eyes,
no appetite
cigarettes, pacing, hyper
always followed by passion,
thinking I'd forgive you.

The lock clears, the bolt turns,
I step into a foreign place,
soiled, dark empty bed,
can't tell, piles of clothes.

Aware I am not alone.

The pit bull growls—
someone else lives here.

IT RINGS

The phone rings and rings—
no answer,
a silent void
on the other end.

You left me after loving.
Wild abandonment,
bite marks still proof.
Gave you what you wanted,

carefully crept to that place.
You never relented,
made me perform, said, "Forever"—
now you're gone.

Went so far into you.
No space, movement,
air we didn't share.

And the phone rings and rings.

SECTION IV

BACKSTAGE

"Let the dead past bury its dead."
(Henry Wadsworth Longfellow)

THE LOFT

In the loft, cinder block barn
among the bales I threw in, stacked.
Yesterday,
a ginger-haired farm boy.

Now, I sit in a concert hall
Gershwin music,
"An American in Paris"—
I was one, a few times.

Walking the Rue Napoleon
reminds me of the gravel road
to the barn
where the cows were jailed.

Their heads in the bars of the stanchion,
eating, being milked.
Of the tree house in the woods
Ricky and I built
to escape,
hang out, make love.
School boys, endless talk
of days ahead.

He gave up all those, me—
for bars like the cows.
He milks away the hours
jailed in a dark bucket of night.

IF THE MORNING COULD CHANGE

The night covered in rain,
darkness, lightning bolts.
Slipped out the window
across the roof, down the gutter spout.

Drenched, walking
miles down the road.
A hay barn, get away
my only hope, my only plan.

Marty lived nearby.
He was the one
who touched me most.
What would he say, do,
I needed to know.

He hugged me,
pulled me inside. Blanket.
in front of the fire,
wet clothes on the floor.

We settled together.
Told him my plan, wondered
would he ask me to stay.
An adult, he

would be punished, jailed.
All that could wait
for the morning after love.

Morning would bring
police, my mother.
Lied to protect him,
my broken heart.

She, the reason I left.
Screen door kicked off the hinges,
beaten for covering up for her.
Her indiscretions.
And yet Marty left alone.
He would be alone for years.
I'm left to remember, wonder
what that morning
might have been.

I TRIED TO TELL YOU

I didn't tell my brother
the night I woke, a hand on my mouth,
lips on my ear, "Be quiet.
Relax. Enjoy. Eat the moment."
Hands rubbing
away my childhood,
moving me into manhood.

My brother's best friend
sleeping over
but not in my brother's bed.

Afraid of the secret I kept.
He wouldn't tell my brother,
betray himself.
Later, my heart beating—
him against me
I shrank, afraid.

He stayed over often,
always ended up in my bed
in the middle of the night.
My brother unaware.

I don't think my brother knew
his friend wasn't there for him.
Silence not to be broken,
no talk of such things.

I tried to tell my brother
at school.
Maybe he did know—
he hit me in the face,
broke my nose.

I lay on the polished gym floor,
blood pooling,
like the side of the road
laying in blood and snot.

I'd never tell him,
never get his help.
I was better off, safer
in the arms of his friend.

THE YEAR OF REPENTANCE

They said it was the year of the Rat or Goat or
some other animal,
that year of Repentance.

It started easily enough, falling into sin, my
descent—
a twisted mix of betrayal and ecstasy

followed, always followed by remorse, agony.

Then the cutting started, I knew I had not
escaped.

No true secrets, no perfect murders
or sins that go unnamed.

EPILOGUE

TO THE LIGHT

"The weak can never forgive. Forgiveness is the attribute of the strong."
(Mahatma Gandhi)

TOMORROW IS HERE

My garden,
sunlight swirls down on me.
My hands in soil,
mind free,
a vine climbing to a place of peace.
No roaring pain, deadly whispers.

Abuse seems far away, powerless.
I feel a great gulf behind me,
a passage from the darkness
of betrayal, abuse,
abandonment—
a place of unforgiveness.

Thin ice, I crossed it.
Dark waters beneath
did not claim me.
Broke through a few times,
but John and Jacob or
trusted others offered
a hand of strength.

Dark the night. It labors on.
I too plod
toward the dawn
away from darkness.

Sometimes I wake,
the light reminds me
no more bruises,
belts,
bleeding or blind rages.

I look back at the darkness,
knew I had to save myself,
know
I'll never inhabit
that unforgiving place.

That moment
working in the dirt,
I find forgiveness. I
made it to the light,
love,
hope and happiness.

Dark stones I carried
cast along the road,
giving me
brighter skies, laughter,
birdsong,
happier days.

ABOUT THE AUTHOR

Willis McCree was born in rural Western Kentucky and grew up on a farm. He served in the Kentucky Army National Guard, received the Kentucky Commendation Award, and was honorably released.

From lighthearted interaction with friends whom he loves to cook for to dark, painful poetry exploring another side of himself to photographic projects, something is always happening in his creative world.

He previously published *When Friends Come Over*, a cookbook inspired by those who spend so much time in the kitchen they never get to visit with friends and family before the meal.

www.ingramcontent.com/pod-product-compliance
Lightning Source LLC
Chambersburg PA
CBHW031415040426
42444CB00005B/578